COGNITIVE BEHAVIORAL THERAPY FOR DEPRESSION

Retrain your Brain from Wrong Behaviors, Irrational Beliefs and Negative Ways of Thinking, Open Yourself to Life, Happiness, and the Freedom of Change

John Rich

Contents

Introduction

The power of thought and the mind have long been recognized by many cultures, religions, and philosophers for hundreds, if not thousands of years. Long before practices mirroring modern psychology came into play, people were using the power of their minds to create happier, healthier lives. A great example of this comes from Buddhism, where monks have been meditating and using their minds to create positive moods, healthier perspectives, and a happier way of life for themselves in general.

It's not just Buddhism, either. Christian people, Jewish people, Islamic people, and people who followed countless philosophers in the early times as well all recognized the power of the human mind. For a long time, the human mind was believed to be our superpower as it has access to levels of thought, awareness, and cognition that exceed virtually any other living species on earth that we know about.

The concept of using your mind to heal something like depression is certainly not new. However, we do have a lot more concrete of an understanding around why it works, how it works, and what you can do to make it work for you in your own life. As you learn how to use modern psychology to heal your own depression, and anxiety if you have it as well, you will likely find that one of the most well-recognized forms of therapy is called Cognitive Behavioral Therapy or "CBT." CBT is not the only form of psychological therapy available to help f people overcome and heal from depression, but it is one of the most powerful and impactful ones out there.

Learning to use CBT in your own life can help you identify how you can begin to change the way you feel by changing the way you think. By using the mindfulness techniques associated with CBT and various other practices associated with this therapy, you will likely find yourself experiencing massive changes in your own ability to manage, cope with, and heal depression in your life.

The practice of CBT, as you will learn about within this very book, was developed in the Western world by a psychology doctor at a university in the United States. However, the practices that contribute to the creation and effectiveness of CBT are largely rooted in Eastern philosophy and are based on practices that have been used for thousands of years by the Eastern world.

As you read through this book, I encourage you to keep an open mind and apply these techniques intentionally and with curiosity as to how they might work for you. As you work toward healing your depression, an open mind will support you heavily in being able to create the state of receptivity that you need in order to actually be able to implement any form of mindfulness or mindset changes in your life. If you attempt to navigate this book with a closed mind, you are going to find yourself denying the effectiveness of the practices before you even try which ultimately means that you will have an incredibly hard time changing your mind. If you cannot change your mind, then you cannot change your life, which means that CBT will not work for you. As you go through this book, be willing to see how each practice might help you and how you might be able to get the most out of it. That way, you can feel confident that you are getting the most out of CBT in general.

In addition to going through this book with an open mind, I also encourage you to find yourself a journal and a pen to go along with it, as there will be plenty that you want to write down. Keeping track of your thoughts, feelings, experiences, and any interesting things you learn about along the way will help you turn the process of healing your depression into a journey that you can appreciate. This way, you can see just how far you have come and how much improvement you have actually made in your life, which can be incredibly inspiring and uplifting when you are working on creating change in your life. It will also help you begin to make sense of the concepts that you are learning about.

If you are ready to begin to learn about what CBT is, how it works, how you can implement it in your own life, and how you can begin naturally healing from depression, it's time to begin. Please read on, and remember, take your time and be patient. Healing from depression can be challenging and can come with many setbacks and slow growth, but it is possible. Stay committed, trust in yourself and in the process, and be prepared to witness a miracle in yourself and in your life experiences!

Chapter 1: Understanding Cognitive Behavioral Therapy

In life, we do not always have the power to change our circumstances or the situations that we find ourselves in. Sometimes, we have very little control over what goes on in our lives, and it can lead to a deep sense of powerlessness, depression, and anxiety. While you cannot always change the world around you, you can change the way that you think about your circumstances so that you begin to feel more empowered, hopeful, and confident within yourself. This entire idea is the foundation of CBT and how this particular model of psychological therapy works.

What is CBT?

CBT was developed as a research-based treatment that can be used to heal many different mood and anxiety disorders that people might deal with in their lives, including depression. This particular therapy method combines cognitive and behavioral methods and has a background of science and scientific literature proving the effectiveness of this method. It has been used to treat depression, eating disorders, anxiety, and other conditions that are rooted in the mind.

The central belief of CBT is that people view situations through a specific cognitive framework that is predetermined by their past experiences and situations. Through that, they cultivate specific thoughts, and those thoughts lead to feelings. When a person reaches the point where they begin experiencing feelings, they will find that those feelings are either pleasant or unpleasant depending on what the feelings themselves are. Sometimes, when those feelings are particularly unpleasant, they can lead to things like depression and anxiety, which can lead to a feeling of distress, hopelessness, or fear within the individual suffering. This is where CBT comes in, as it focuses on helping the individual change their perspective by changing their thoughts so that their feelings follow suit, too.

How Does CBT Work?

This central belief is promoted by the idea of how emotions are created within the human body. While there is still no concrete findings that confirm exactly how emotions are created, the commonly accepted understanding is that emotions are actually our physiological reactions to our thoughts. So, an individual starts by being exposed to certain circumstances or situations, and through that, they cultivate a series of thoughts about those circumstances or situations. The thoughts that each person has will depend on their cognitive framework, or their previous experiences which ultimately shape what they are most likely to focus on in their circumstances or situations, and how they are likely to focus on that information. Once the thoughts have been formulated, the individual forms a perception of their reality based on those thoughts, which leads to the production of emotions. Emotions, then, are meant to help the individual navigate those experiences in a way that is appropriate based on their perception of reality. So, let's say someone is in an environment that they perceive as being exciting and joyful, and so they begin to experience excitement and joy. These feelings would help them remain open and receptive to the environment while also having the energy to engage in and interact with it. If they were in an environment where they perceived threats or danger, however, they would experience the emotion of fear which would enable them to have the proper energy and mental abilities to stay focused and protect themselves.

When someone's cognitive framework is leading to them continually recognizing certain parts of their circumstances or situations that lead to feelings of depression or anxiety, then we can conclude that the cognitive framework is off. Rather than supporting that individual in experiencing their environment, they will find themselves experiencing unexplainable, unrealistic, or unnecessary emotions in response to their environment instead. When this happens, something needs to be done to change the framework so that the individual can begin to see the environment realistically and accurately again, thus allowing them to experience a healthy spectrum of emotional expression again.

The History of CBT

CBT was recognized and developed in the 1950s and 1960s by two different psychologists: Dr. Albert Ellis and Dr. Aaron T. Beck. With that being said, it is often recognized as being Aaron T. Beck's development, and Dr. Ellis is often left out of the picture, which is an inaccurate representation of who actually developed and introduced CBT to the world.

Dr. Ellis was originally a person who stood strongly behind the theory of classical psychoanalysis but, over time, lost faith in the method and it's effectiveness. Ellis found himself fascinated by ancient philosophy, particularly the concept of Stoicism and decided to focus his efforts on creating a therapy that harnessed some of the concepts of these philosophies. From these efforts, he started helping patients begin to understand their own irrational beliefs so that they could ultimately restructure the ones that were leading to feelings of emotional suffering. This approach became so refined over time that it actually became its own form of therapy which became known in psychology as "Rational Emotive Behavioral Therapy" (REBT.) This particular form of therapy is not identical to CBT, but it does have many similarities that enable it to reinforce the validity of CBT.

Around the same time that Ellis was creating and trying out REBT, Dr. Aaron T. Beck conducted research with Ellis that supported this new concept. In his understanding, they were engaging in "cognitive therapy" that worked with the cognitive functions within people's brains. He combined the understandings learned for REBT with his own findings to create and "found" cognitive behavioral therapy, which is why he is recognized as the single founder. Despite that, it can be understood that Ellis played a large role in Beck reaching this point and identifying CBT, and they both offer excellent findings and cases to explain the power of cognitive therapies.

Beck had also been a proponent for classical psychoanalysis, but like Ellis, he was looking for new approaches when he ultimately discovered that his own findings and research failed to validate the concepts of classical psychoanalysis. Through this, he found that actively engaging with patients and bringing them into the process of healing through identifying their own negative thoughts and developing more rational belief systems supported them in overcoming emotional suffering. More specifically, it supported them in overcoming depression in his earliest findings, and anxiety and other mood disorders and mental illnesses in later findings.

Through their research and findings, both Beck and Ellis discovered that thoughts and beliefs are the true causes of depression, anxiety, and other mood disorders and mental illnesses that are rooted within the mind. People who experience mislead or distorted cognitive frameworks find themselves experiencing things like depression and anxiety frequently and, when supported with CBT, often find themselves completely overcoming their symptoms altogether.

One of the most revolutionary parts of their findings was that Beck and Ellis discovered that the key to helping people overcome things like depression was actually to involve patients in their therapy, rather than trying to heal them without their assistance. They realized that patients were not suffering from no known cause, they simply could not understand why their own thoughts were misfiring the way they were and leading to depression in many cases. If a therapist could work with them to identify problematic thoughts and beliefs, however, then they could use that as the groundwork for creating changes in the thought processes which would ultimately help the individual overcome their symptoms.

CBT-based therapists and CBT-based approaches focus less on why something is happening and more on what can be done about the problems a person is facing. In this, you can understand that the purpose of CBT is more focused on building effective skills that can be developed, practiced, and applied to a patient's entire life, rather than just within the therapist's office. This way, the individual could become more resilient and healthy in the everyday world, which ultimately leads to a greater likelihood of them being able to combat and overcome their ailments.

The skills that CBT will support an individual with include all of those that surround their ability to heighten their sense of self-awareness, especially pertaining to emotional self-awareness. When an individual has increased awareness of their own thoughts and emotions, they become far more capable of identifying how different situations and circumstances are influencing their thoughts and behaviors. They also begin to understand how their thoughts and behaviors are leading to the emotions they are experiencing, which ultimately leads to them being able to identify and modify dysfunctional or problematic thoughts and behaviors. This way, they can intentionally begin to experience more pleasurable and purposeful thoughts and behaviors that lead to feelings and emotions that are far more manageable, as well.

What CBT Can Help With

Cognitive Behavioral Therapy has the capacity to help with many things. Depression was the original purpose of CBT, and it is also the primary focus of this very book. However, CBT can also help with other mood disorders or mental illnesses that people may experience. For example, anxiety is another big thing that CBT can help people overcome, and I go into greater detail on how and why in my book *Cognitive Behavioral Therapy for Anxiety*. In addition to anxiety, it can help with phobias, eating disorders, and even the mental and emotional aspects that may come with facing severe illnesses or their side effects, or even one's own mortality.

How CBT Differs From Other Depression Therapies and Treatments

CBT is different from other forms of depression therapies and treatments because it largely focuses on empowering the individual suffering to recognize how they can take back control over their own mental landscape. By showing an individual how they can adjust their thinking and rebuild their cognitive framework to create a mindset that fosters more pleasant emotions and experiences, depression, and other such ailments can be overcome.

Other forms of therapy tend to focus heavily on treating the root cause, medicating the depression, treating it indirectly, or ignoring the causes and symptoms of depression while attempting to harness healthier day-to-day habits. Some of these alternative therapies include: classical psychoanalysis, various medications, dietary and lifestyle changes, and positivity washing or attempting to "think positive" to heal the problem. While these other methods can certainly aid in the healing and recovery of depression, they are not generally effective in completely healing depression. Often, they lead to the depression getting worse, the person feeling hopeless, or the person becoming reliant on a healing method that may not necessarily help for a long period of time. If they find themselves incapable of accessing that healing method or it no longer working, the individual is once again exposed to depression and emotional suffering because they lack the foundational skills to change it.

By embracing CBT and everything it teaches, people are able to begin changing the way they face their emotional experiences by creating skills that can be used again and again. Over time, these skills strengthen and the person will find themselves having a stronger ability to adapt to and overcome the various circumstances and situations they face in their lives without experiencing so much emotional distress. To summarize, CBT is about healing the problem, rather than attempting to passively heal the cause or manage the symptoms. This way, a person can feel confident that they are actually going to be able to overcome any future bout of depression they may experience, too, rather than living in fear of another major episode coming on and them not being able to navigate it. Since depression can lead to suicidal thoughts, tendencies, and attempts, feeling confident in your capacity to manage depression is crucial if you are going to be able to maintain your wellbeing and prevent yourself from feeling unsafe within your own body.

Chapter 2: Alternatives to Cognitive Behavioral Therapy

Since the discovery of CBT and REBT, many other psychologists and doctors have gone on to study these forms of therapies and create their own alternatives to CBT, too. It appears that when Beck and Ellis discovered the power of the cognitive mind, everyone realized that this was the most effective way forward and decided to put it to the test. As a result, a few other forms of therapy were developed that follow a similar framework and lead to the healing of depression and other mood disorders, too.

The four most commonly recognized alternatives to CBT include REBT, Dialectical Behavioral Therapy (DBT), Exposure and Response Prevention Therapy (ERP), and Acceptance and Commitment Therapy (ACT).

Although this book is not going to teach you how to use these alternative therapies, we will discuss what they are and how they work. Recognizing that they work on a similar framework as CBT might help you recognize the power of CBT itself and the capacity it has to support you in healing from depression. As well, if you find that certain concepts in CBT do not make sense or do not seem to help you as much as you wish, you can always look into these alternatives and create a combination approach to support you in healing from your depression. At the end of the day, the most important thing is that you find what works for you and that you apply it consistently so that you can develop the necessary skills, strength, and resiliency to overcome your depression.

Rational Emotive Behavioral Therapy (REBT)

REBT is a form of psychotherapy that supports individuals in identifying their self-defeating thoughts and feelings. After they have identified these self-defeating thoughts and feelings, they are then guided to challenge the rationality of those feelings and choose to replace them with a healthier and more productive system of beliefs. In this way, people are encouraged to see that not everything they think is absolutely true and that they can change their thoughts to experience healthier and more pleasant thoughts and emotions.

When it comes to REBT, the therapy recognizes that people have the capacity to experience unhealthy thoughts and beliefs which can lead to them creating emotional distress within themselves based on these thoughts and beliefs. As a result of this emotional distress, individuals begin to experience unhealthy behaviors and actions that can interfere with their current life goals, as well as their wellbeing. Once an individual can identify and understand why these negative thoughts and beliefs exist, they can take action to change them and replace them with something more positive that will support them with experiencing a healthier way of life. As a result, they will develop more successful personal and professional lives, relationships, and health.

Dialectical Behavioral Therapy (DBT)

DBT is a form of therapy that supports patients in discovering new skills that they can use to help them manage their painful emotions. They can also use these skills to decrease conflict in their relationships so that they are more likely to experience healthier and happier relationships with themselves, their peers, their family and friends, and their romantic partners.

DBT focuses on four key areas where patients are encouraged to build and nurture skills within themselves. These key areas include mindfulness, distress tolerance, emotion regulation, and interpersonal effectiveness. With mindfulness, the individual is taught how they can become more capable of accepting their present reality and staying grounded in the present moment. With distress tolerance, individuals are taught how to increase their tolerance to stressful situations so that they are less likely to experience such massive stress responses. For emotional regulation, people are taught how to regulate their intense emotions so that their emotions are less likely to cause problems in their lives. When it comes to interpersonal effectiveness, patients are taught to communicate in a way with others that is assertive while also maintaining their self-respect and improving the quality of their relationships with others.

Exposure and Response Prevention Therapy (ERP)

Exposure and Response Prevention Therapy have one primary goal when it comes to supporting patients with overcoming their challenges in life. The goal is to support those who are having excessive obsessive thoughts refrain from actually engaging in those thoughts with compulsions or habitual behaviors. ERP focuses on exposing people to things gradually over time while also giving them skills on how to navigate the exposures effectively. This way, their maladaptive responses can be overcome, and they can begin to learn how to navigate their obsessions more intentionally, rather than being taken over by habits and compulsions.

Acceptance and Commitment Therapy (ACT)

The ACT is a form of psychotherapy that is rooted in the practices of traditional CBT but focuses on action-oriented approaches. The goal of ACT is for patients to stop engaging in behaviors of avoidance, denial, and struggling when it comes to their own inner emotions. Rather than experiencing these behaviors, the patient learns to accept these feelings, recognize them as being appropriate responses to the stimuli that caused them, and commit to continuing to move forward in their lives anyway. The goal here is for them to recognize that what they are feeling is normal and natural and that it does not need to hold them back or prevent them from continuing to move forward in life.

Patients of ACT are taught to accept issues and hardships in their lives and commit to making the necessary changes in their behavior so that they can stop feeling victimized by the experiences they have had. They also have to commit to making these changes in their thoughts, feelings, and emotions. The ACT is highly similar to CBT, except that the focus is more on accepting and committing to moving on, whereas the focus of CBT is identifying and committing to change.

Chapter 3: An Overview of Depression

As you have come to this book to help you heal and overcome your depression, it can be helpful for you to take the time to fully understand what depression is and how it is affecting you in your life. Depression is a fairly complex and often overwhelming experience to understand and take on in your life. It can arise for many different reasons, and it can lead to many uncomfortable and frustrating symptoms in your life that can be challenging to navigate and overcome.

The more you understand what depression is, the easier it is for you to understand how depression has been affecting your life and what you should do about it. This is helpful in supporting you with overcoming questions like "what is wrong with me?" and "why can't I just feel good?" or "why can't I just be normal?" When you can overcome these questions with serious and helpful answers, it becomes easier for you to navigate and overcome your depression successfully.

It is important to understand that not every case of depression is the same, so what you read throughout this chapter may or may not be the same as what you are experiencing in your life. You will likely find that you resonate with some of these symptoms and recognize them in your own life and that you do not resonate with others. The more you can recognize this and understand your own depression, however, the better as this will support you in creating a clearer understanding of your own experience and what can be done to help you overcome your unique case of depression. If you want to, this is a great time to start jotting things down in your notebook as you keep track of what symptoms you recognize within yourself so that you can clearly see what you are dealing with inside of yourself as you face your depression.

What is Depression?

Depression is a common medical illness that is recognized as being a serious condition as it can lead to the experience of suicidal thoughts which, if left unmanaged, can become fatal. For that reason, people need to recognize that if they are dealing with depression, they are dealing with a serious and possibly life-threatening mental illness that needs to be addressed promptly and with proper care and concern.

Doctors of all varieties recognize depression as being a form of medical mental illness that leads to negatively affected thoughts, feelings, and behaviors in the people who are facing it. Often, these thoughts, feelings, and behaviors lead to and represent a lack of joy being gained from any activities, a loss of interest in life itself, and feelings of deep inner sadness. It can also lead to several other emotional and physical problems that people may face as secondary symptoms due to their decreased ability to remain functional in their personal and professional lives.

Depression is recognized as being a condition that affects the brain with many probable causes, although there is no single root cause associated with depression. Instead, it could be caused due to many different things, ranging from feeling overwhelmed or stressed out with your day-to-day life to having trouble coping with something major or overwhelming in life. It is also believed that depression can be caused by hormonal or chemical imbalances or by inheriting a predisposition to the disorder.

Who is at Risk of Getting Depression?

Depression has the capacity to affect anyone under any circumstances, even if that person appears to be living a healthy and normal life. Because of how susceptible the entire population seems to be to depression, it is hard to pinpoint any one specific reason as to why people may be at risk of getting depression. With that being said, there are four commonly recognized risk factors that make a person more likely to get depression over anyone else, and having one or more of these risk factors may make you more at risk of experiencing depression yourself. These four risk factors include biochemistry, genetics, personality, and environmental factors.

Biochemistry recognizes that certain chemicals in the brain can contribute to symptoms of depression which may ultimately lead to an individual being affected by depression. This type of depression is often attributed to being caused by a chemical imbalance and may or may not be treatable with proper medications, dietary changes, and lifestyle changes, in general, that support the healthy production of hormones and chemicals in the brain and body. Often, this is the type of depression that people end up using medication as a primary method for treatment, and they can use other things like CBT and lifestyle changes as secondary forms of treatment. The reason why CBT and other psychotherapies alone are not strong enough to treat this type of depression, however, is because it is caused by a chemical imbalance and not a flawed thought process. However, CBT and other similar therapies can still be powerful in providing the sufferer with the necessary skills to overcome the troubling symptoms associated with their depression so they are not as deeply affected. This may also help them navigate particularly troubling experiences that their medications may not be able to support them with.

Genetics is believed to be a factor in people being diagnosed with depression, too. It is believed that if depression runs in your family, you are at risk of inheriting depression as well. One study showed that if one identical twin has depression, there is a 70% chance that the other twin will develop depression at some point, too. Like biochemistry, genetics are a risk factor that cannot necessarily be avoided using CBT or other psychotherapies. With that being said, it can still provide the sufferer with the necessary skills to cope with the difficult symptoms while they work with their medical team to find an appropriate way to heal and overcome their depression. As well, some people who inherit depression do still find incredible relief in healing their depression through CBT.

Personality is said to increase an individual's risk of inheriting depression when the person has a low sense of self-esteem, if they can easily be overwhelmed by stress, or if they have a pessimistic outlook on life. People with these forms of personalities are said to be more at risk because, in CBT terms, their existing cognitive framework is already causing them to look at the unpleasant things in life. If they are not careful, they may completely miss all of the pleasant things, as a result, and through that, they may find themselves experiencing depression. People who become depressed due to their personalities often find incredible relief using forms of therapy like CBT.

Environmental factors can contribute to depression when an individual feels completely out of control of their environment and incapable of doing anything about it. For example, continued exposure to violence, neglect, poverty, or abuse may lead to someone being more vulnerable to depression. With that being said, these are not the only experiences that can affect a person's environment and lead to depression. Environments that are overly stressful or overwhelming can also lead to depression. This type of depression can be navigated best by first identifying what environmental factors are contributing to a person's depression. If they are being negatively impacted by their environment through something dangerous such as violence, abuse, neglect, or poverty, that person will need to do what they can to access safety as well as use tools like CBT to support them in healing. If they are in an environment with a large amount of stress or that feeds their pessimistic point of view, CBT alongside some effective stress-management tools may be enough to support them with overcoming their depression.

What are the Symptoms of Depression?

The number one symptom of depression that most people recognize is the feeling of overwhelming, uncontrollable sadness or having a depressed mood. Sometimes, the individual may not be able to describe their depression as sadness but may instead describe it as feeling "nothingness." This, too, can be a sign that depression is at play and that the person is struggling with symptoms of depression.

Another big sign of someone struggling with depression is feeling disinterested in things that used to be pleasurable or enjoyable for them. Or, if the depression is, further along, feeling disinterested in doing anything at all. Some people who are struggling with more advanced or severe forms of depression may struggle to even take care of their basic needs like brushing their teeth, getting enough nutrition, or getting to work on a daily basis.

In addition to struggling with taking care of themselves, they may find that they have an irregular sleep cycle and an irregular appetite. A person with depression may sleep too much, or struggle to sleep at all. Likewise, they might eat too much, or struggle to eat at all. They may also find themselves losing energy in general or constantly feeling fatigued even if they are not tired enough to actually sleep.

Physically, a person who is struggling with depression may find their movements slowing down and may find themselves struggling with staying active. They may physically walk or move slower, talk slower, or generally behave slower compared to usual.

This may not be as recognizable to them as it is to others, although they may feel on some level that they are moving slower and they may think it's just due to tiredness.

In their minds, people with depression often experience thoughts of being worthless or guilty about something, even when they have nothing to be guilty about. They may feel guilty that their lack of motivation and energy is hurting the people around them, even if it isn't, because of their distorted perception of reality. They may also have difficulty thinking, as well as difficulty concentrating, and making decisions may be too challenging for them. In some cases, people with depression may also think or feel suicidal or have frequent thoughts of death to the point where they romanticize death in their minds.

In order to be classified as clinical depression, a person must have these symptoms for at least two weeks. However, if you have symptoms associated with suicidal thoughts or death, this is a strong sign that you are dealing with depression, and you should not wait for a diagnosis to seek and begin treatment.

Are There Different Types of Depression?

Depression does not just come in one shape or size, which is why not everyone will have the same symptoms when they experience depression. There are actually nine different types of depression according to Web MD, each of which includes their own unique symptoms and their own unique causes and treatments. These nine types of depression include major depression, persistent depressive disorder, bipolar disorder, seasonal affective disorder

(SAD), psychotic depression, peripartum (postpartum) depression, premenstrual dysphoric disorder (PMDD), situational depression, and atypical depression.

Major depression is characterized by an individual who feels depressed more often than not, and who experiences these symptoms on an ongoing basis for two weeks or longer. A persistent depressive disorder is recognized in patients who have depression for longer than 2 years and used to be called dysthymia. Bipolar disorder is also sometimes called manic depression, and it is characterized by times of extreme highs (mania) and extreme lows (depression.) Seasonal affective disorder or SAD affects people when the weather changes and occurs most frequently in the wintertime when there is less sunlight. Psychotic depression is when an individual experiences depression combined with symptoms of psychosis such as hallucinations, delusions, and paranoia. Peripartum (postpartum) depression occurs in women in the weeks and months following childbirth and may start prior to the child actually being born. Premenstrual dysphoric disorder (PMDD) occurs in women at the start of their period and includes symptoms reflecting depression that do not last past the length of their period. Situational depression is not an official medical term, but it reflects depression that occurs as a result of someone's situation, such as when you are managing an incredibly stressful life event. Atypical depression is a form of depression that means that you have depression but positive events or experiences can temporarily improve your mood, whereas other forms of depression are not changed by the events you experience.

Are Depression and Anxiety Related?

Believe it or not, depression and anxiety are closely related and the symptoms can sometimes be hard to tell apart. Often, when a patient goes in to speak with their psychiatrist or psychologist, they believe they have one when, in reality, they have the other. This is because anxiety and depression can both lead to similar feelings of demotivation, fatigue, overwhelm, and an unwillingness to partake in your life. The key difference is that people who are depressed do not want to participate because they lack motivation or energy, whereas people who are anxious do not want to participate because they are anxious and overwhelmed.

The process of identifying which you are struggling with, or which is most bothersome in your life, can be challenging, however, as one can often lead to the other. For example, if you are depressed and you lack the motivation or energy to do anything but you have to do it anyway, you may begin to feel anxious because you are aware of the fact that you lack the energy. This may make you believe that you are dealing with anxiety when, in fact, you are dealing with depression. Alternatively, if you need to get something done but you are feeling too scared to get it done so you procrastinate, you may think you are depressed because you lack the motivation when, in reality, you are avoiding that task due to anxiety.

While these two conditions are different and do come with different symptoms and causes, many people find that they experience both at the same time. If this is the case for you, you are going to want to treat both your depression and your anxiety at the same time so that you can begin to heal yourself from both. This way, you are more likely to experience a complete resolve from the mood disorders that are affecting you.

The positive thing about dealing with both depression and anxiety, or one or the other, is that they both have a similar approach to treatment. For both of these disorders, CBT can be incredibly helpful in assisting you with overcoming the thought processes that lead to the unwanted symptoms that you have been experiencing.

How Does One Face and Heal Depression?

Facing and healing depression is no easy feat, but it is one that can be accomplished. One of the biggest keys to facing and healing depression is being willed to have hope and trust that it is possible. Because one of the most common symptoms of depression *is* feelings of hopelessness and powerlessness, it can be incredibly challenging for you to create feelings of hope and trust. However, if you can focus on hoping and trusting that there is a solution, you are well on your way to letting these solutions work for you so that you can begin to face and overcome your depression.

In addition to being hopeful and trusting that it is possible, you also need to be willing to look for the ways that work for you. As I said, depression can be caused by many things, and everyone's experience with depression is going to be unique based on the symptoms they are having, the reasons why, and the treatment methods that work best for them. When you are facing and healing depression, you need to be willing to try different methods of treatment until you find the methods that work best for you. Then, you will find yourself being able to completely overcome your depression and move forward with a stronger mind, body, and soul.

As you do begin to find your unique treatment methods, I strongly advise you to take the power of CBT and psychotherapy into consideration, even if you do find that you need to use medications or other treatments in addition to CBT. Unlike other treatment methods, CBT will give you the skills you need to navigate the symptoms, which is powerful whether it is used on its own or combined with other treatment methods. Knowing how to cope could be the difference between being able to stay in control long enough to get medical intervention or not for some people, which, in many cases, can be the difference between life and death. No matter how serious or seemingly minor your depression is, having these skills will be wildly helpful for you when you are facing and overcoming your depression.

Chapter 4: Negativity Bias and Your Brain

As we begin to explore deeper into CBT and the cognitive framework that leaves you vulnerable to depression, one thing we really need to take a look at is negativity bias. Negativity bias can massively affect people's psyche and lead to them being far more pessimistic and depressed or anxious than they reasonably think they should be, and it all happens for a natural reason.

Many people are completely unaware of the fact that they are affected by negativity bias which can lead to them feeling like they are constantly being negative and without any clear understanding as to why or how this is happening. Often, this can lead to them feeling overwhelmed and like there may be something wrong with them because they are struggling to engage in healthy, positive thoughts. Especially if they see people around them being optimistic and positive, they may find themselves feeling even more stressed out or overwhelmed by their negativity bias. When people find out that everyone faces this and that it is natural, it often helps them calm down and feel more at peace with their experiences and more willing to attempt to navigate and overcome them.

Another benefit of understanding negativity bias is realizing that even seemingly minor negative experiences do have a fairly large impact on the brain. When you begin to understand the impact of negative experiences on your life, it becomes easier for you to recognize why these negative experiences are happening and what you can do about it.

What is Negativity Bias?

Negativity bias is a phenomenon that occurs naturally in the human brain, and it works by having the human psyche become more affected by negative experiences than it does positive experiences of equal magnitude. So, if you were to experience something that was negative, then experience something that was the equal amount except positive, you would be more likely to have your psyche impressed upon by the negative experience. This means that you could have an incredibly positive experience, and slightly negative experience and both would leave the same level of impression on your brain.

Negativity bias has been investigated by many different types of psychologists, doctors, and researchers. Still, the entirety of it and everything it does to affect the brain is not completely understood. However, most agree that it exists and agree that its purpose is to serve in survival and evolution. Ideally, if the negativity bias is working properly, you will be more likely to remember things that have negatively affected your survival or wellbeing and you will be able to avoid them in the future. This way, you are less likely to be exposed to things that pose a threat to you, even if the threat is minor or non-existent.

How Negativity Bias Affects Your Brain

Negativity bias can affect your brain in many different ways. It largely affects your cognition and decision-making skills, however, as it deeply affects that part of your brain in many ways. One big way that negativity bias affects your brain is through negative experiences demanding more energy and processing than positive experiences, which results in you having to exert more energy and effort into actually navigating negative experiences. These differences can be seen on a neurological level and show that the negativity bias can actually impact attention, learning, and memory.

Your attention is affected because negativity is essentially an attention magnet, which means that your brain is always going to focus on the negative in your life. Again, the purpose here is that if anything in the negative areas of your life become a threat to your wellbeing, you will be aware of them and ready to navigate them so that you can survive.

For learning and memory, the purpose is the same. If you are able to remain aware of negativity and danger, you are able to react to it quicker. You are also able to learn about that possible threat and recall it so that, in future experiences, it is no longer a risk for you. From a survival standpoint, this is a large part of human evolution: the ability to remember and use previous negative experiences to prevent future negative experiences. If we do not take the time to learn to navigate our negativity bias and use it mindfully, however, it can lead to incredible stress and overwhelm on an almost constant basis.

Because of how negativity bias can affect your attention, learning, and memory, it can also affect your decision-making process. All of this combined leads to you experiencing a unique cognitive framework that leads to you having a hard time effectively perceiving situations without a negative connotation. As a result, you might find yourself making decisions solely based on memories and past experiences, rather than on rational reasoning and logical thinking. While this is not so bad when your frameworks are healthy and functioning properly, if they begin to become imbalanced, they can lead to you having difficulty experiencing healthy thoughts and, therefore, healthy emotions and behaviors, too.

Negativity Bias and Depression

Because of how negativity bias works, you can understand that it can play a large contribution to people developing depression in their lives. With the continuous natural focus on the negative things and the intense impact that negative things can have on us in our lives, it can be easy for us to get swept up in negativity bias and find ourselves struggling to get beyond it.

When negativity bias takes over in your life and you have no healthy coping methods for how to heal from the negative experiences or create more positive experiences in your life, it can be challenging. You might find yourself feeling at odds with your mind and with your mood because you cannot find ways to overcome the negative stuff naturally. As a result, you find yourself feeling increasingly more negative and, therefore, more depressed.

If you want to reduce your likelihood of experiencing depression as a result of negativity bias, you need to create space for yourself to become aware of and overcome your negativity bias. The more you can be mindful of how this behavior impacts you, the more you can start controlling it so that it no longer has such an intense impact on you in your life.

Can Negativity Bias Be Overcome?

Based on the very nature of what negativity bias is and how it works, you cannot necessarily heal your negativity bias or stop it from existing. However, you can learn ways to cope with and overcome your negativity bias so that it stops affecting you so significantly. Learning how to overcome your negativity bias will help you learn the healthy coping methods that prevent negativity bias from being so controlling in your life, which essentially means that you will begin to change the cognitive framework. As a result, you will find yourself experiencing negativity bias in a more objective way, rather than in such an intense and overwhelming way. From this, you will likely find yourself suffering less from the pessimistic tendencies that negativity bias can lead to.

There are three really important steps you can use to help you overcome negativity bias which is actually also effective in CBT as well. Essentially, anything you can do to help you change your experience is going to help you change your thoughts which will change your behavior and emotions, and therefore, serve in changing your cognitive behavioral experience.

The three steps that you need to use to overcome negativity bias include supporting your experiences with facts, savoring experiences, and taking the time to mindfully experience good things in your life. When you support your experiences with facts, you allow yourself the ability to become realistic about your experiences and stop seeing the negative quite so intently. This way, you can honestly recount your experiences in life rather than seeing everything as negative and horrible. When you allow yourself to savor the experience, and to let the good experience sink in, you allow that feeling to impress upon your subconscious mind more effectively. This way, your positive experiences start to feel just as impactful as your negative experiences, which helps you recognize that your life is not entirely filled with negative experiences. As you begin to learn how to use and navigate CBT, you will find that it becomes a lot easier for you to engage in these three practices to overcome your negativity bias, too. This way, you can start creating a strong cognitive framework for you to have a healthy, positive experience, rather than an overwhelming and consistently negative one.

Chapter 5: Learning to Understand Yourself and Your Depression

Before you can really dig into healing your depression, you need to increase your level of self-awareness and understanding within yourself. The more you can understand yourself and your inner world, the more you are going to find yourself understanding why you are experiencing depression and what aspects of yourself are being affected by depression.

Getting to know yourself from within your depression, particularly if you have never gotten to know yourself well outside of your depression, might feel challenging. At times, it can be difficult to discern what is an aspect of your real personality and what is an aspect of your depression. You might find yourself questioning what is you, and what is your depression, sometimes to the point where you struggle to discern and feel balanced in following your truth. However, the more you get to know yourself and the more you practice criticizing your automatic thoughts, the more you are going to find yourself getting to know who you truly are. Over time, you will find yourself naturally understanding and identifying your true self and being able to tell the difference between who you are and what your depression is.

Once you begin to tell the difference between yourself and your depression, you will find yourself naturally and easily creating space for you to start finding ways to overcome your depression. The pursuit, at that point, will ultimately be between the truth (who you really are) and the depression (the symptoms you are having.) Using CBT and other natural methods, you will be able to start identifying with and aligning yourself toward your true self and true beliefs, rather than the false self and false beliefs you have been associating with due to depression.

The Importance of Self-Awareness and Understanding Yourself

When it comes to depression, some of the thought processes people have can be incredibly tricky. People often find themselves thinking thoughts as a symptom of depression and ultimately believing those thoughts to be true. This belief can lead to the individual feeling as though they are bad, wrong, worthless, hopeless, helpless, or otherwise in a negative space. It can also lead to them believing that there is no chance for this to change and that they will always feel bad. In extreme cases, these symptomatic thought processes can lead to the individual toying with the idea of suicide and genuinely believing that they must commit suicide in order to save themselves or other people in their lives.

When an individual is unaware of the difference between themselves and their real thoughts and their depression and their depressive thoughts, they can begin to identify with their depression. As a result, they may find themselves struggling to understand who they are and what their depression is, which can lead to overwhelming and destructive experiences.

As you learn how to develop self-awareness and understand yourself and your symptoms as being two separate things, it becomes easier for you to recognize when you are experiencing depression. This way, you can allow yourself to stop identifying as and internalizing your depressive symptomatic thoughts. Although this will not cause them to stop happening altogether, nor will it lead to them being any less painful or overwhelming, it will help you begin to recognize that they are not ultimately true. From this space, you begin to cultivate a deeper sense of safety and wellbeing as well as a deeper sense of understanding around what is true and what is a symptom of your illness.

You can begin to cultivate self-awareness by allowing yourself to start criticizing your thoughts and feelings from a place that ultimately questions how true they are. When you are intensely depressed, it might be hard to answer these questions of criticism honestly, but as you continue practicing and trying, you will likely find that it becomes easier for you.

The questions of criticism that you need to ask yourself include "Do I ultimately believe this to be true?" "Is this really me?" "Are there other beliefs that I can have that are more nurturing and gentle on myself?" and "How can I believe those more gentle thoughts?"

Often, you will find that when you are experiencing depression, you are able to rationalize that you do not ultimately believe the depressive thoughts and that they do not accurately reflect who you really are. You can also begin to back this up with evidence if you need to so that you can begin to validate to yourself that your beliefs are not ultimately true. Then, you can begin to identify which other beliefs may be more honest and accurate and start to look for ways that you can begin to naturally and completely believe in these other beliefs. Once you can begin to create this rationality in your mind, you can begin to look for space where CBT can be applied for you to begin making real changes in your depressive experiences.

Understanding Your Own Depression by Tracking Your Own Symptoms

As you get to know yourself and cultivate a sense of self-awareness, you need to start tracking your depressive symptoms and experiences so that you can start understanding what depression is like for you. Remember, depression is not the same for everyone so you may not have all of the same symptoms, experiences, or thought processes as the other people in your life. The more you can recognize what your own depression looks like, the easier it is going to be for you to start working on making yourself better from your depressive experiences.

The first thing you can do to start understanding your own depression is tracking your own symptoms. In your journal, every time you experience a depressive thought or episode, a strange sleep cycle, an unusual appetite experience, or anything else related to depression track it. Write down as much as you can about this experience so that you are always clear on what is happening around this particular symptom. This will be important in helping you track your patterns and recognize your symptoms, as well as possibly predict them in the future.

An example of what you should be writing down when you track your symptoms includes what the symptom is (in detail,) what was happening immediately before it started, what happened during the symptom's experience, and when the experience subsided and if it did. If the experience does subside, also make sure that you write down what happened when it subsided, in case your actions are in some way supporting you in overcoming your symptoms.

Being able to track your symptoms and depressive experiences more completely ensures that you are able to begin to track and understand patterns in your symptoms. This way, you can begin to create a clear understanding of what might be causing these symptoms and what these symptoms might be leading to. You will also begin to recognize what types of things tend to help you feel better or at least partially lift some of your symptoms through these patterns, too.

Ideally, you should track your symptoms every single day that you feel depressed, no matter how many times you have experienced depression or how many times it has come back for you. However, at the very least, you should track your symptoms for 3-5 days to start getting a clearer understanding of what your depression is, how it works, and how it feels for you.

You should always look back on your symptom tracking sheets after you have been tracking for a while to see if you can recognize any patterns or unique points in your depression. The more you can allow yourself to understand what is causing your depression, and what depression looks and feels like for you, the more you are going to be able to develop a self-awareness that separates you from your depression. This way, you can start to recognize when you are experiencing symptoms which will be essential in helping you pinpoint your unhelpful thoughts and treat them using CBT.

Understanding What Helps You Feel Better

As you track your symptoms, it is always a good idea to look at tracking what helps you feel better, too. The more you can understand both your depression *and* what helps you manage, cope with, or treat your depression, the more you are going to find yourself being able to find ways to cope with and heal your depression. Because we do all experience depression differently, understanding yourself and your own experiences and treatments mean that you have the opportunity to recognize where your cognitive frameworks lie and how it's impacting your wellness.

Understanding what helps you feel better is ultimately going to help you in two very important ways when it comes to healing your depression. First, it will help you recognize what you can do to treat your depression naturally, and second, it will help you identify where you can begin to treat yourself using CBT as it will allow you to recognize your thought patterns and what typically feels better for you.

When it comes to recognizing what you can do to treat your depression naturally, you will likely find that there are certain activities, behaviors, or experiences that tend to help lighten or lift your mood. Recognizing these activities, behaviors, and experiences allows you to begin identifying how you can create a deeper sense of wellness in your life by making space for these behaviors. You can engage in them on a regular basis to help lighten your mood overall, while also using them during particularly low times to help support you in creating a better mood overall.

It is important to understand that most activities or practices you try, including CBT, are not always going to feel great at first. At first, you might find yourself aimlessly engaging in these behaviors with the feeling that what you are doing is hopeless and will not be able to help you feel any better. However, you will likely find that as you remain committed to that experience and you keep allowing yourself to engage in it regardless of how you feel at the time, you start feeling better over time. This is common as depression can cause a deep sense of disconnect from what you are doing and your feelings, so do not fret if you find yourself engaging in something and not feeling better right away. Commit to doing it and you will likely see results over time.

Aside from helping you understand what behaviors and practices help you feel better, tracking what helps you feel better is also going to help you identify what thoughts and beliefs tend to help you feel better, too. When it comes to CBT, a large part of what you will be doing is redirecting your mind to recognize new thoughts and beliefs that feel more whole and nurturing for you. The more you can identify what beliefs and thoughts help you feel better, the more you are going to be able to identify ways that you can combat your negative or unhelpful thoughts with these positive, helpful thoughts.

When it comes to CBT, you truly will need to practice finding thoughts and beliefs that fit you and your needs. It can be easy to explain what CBT is and how it works, as well as what helpful thoughts and beliefs are, however, if you do not genuinely believe in those thoughts and beliefs, it is going to be hard for you to embody them. Finding helpful redirections that you can genuinely get behind will be important in helping CBT truly work for you so that you can start to redirect your thoughts in a way that you can truly get behind.

Chapter 6: The Process of Cognitive Behavioral Therapy for Depression

Applying CBT to depression specifically is unique from applying it to other practices. While the general process looks the same, you will find that the way that it works and what happens as you begin applying it looks somewhat different since your symptoms with depression are unique from any other symptoms in your life.

In this chapter, we are going to explore what CBT looks like for depression specifically so that you can begin to identify how CBT is going to help you overcome your depression. Understand that the following guidelines are helpful in supporting you with understanding how CBT will work, but they will not exactly identify what it is going to look like for you. Just as depression is different from person to person, so too is treatment, so while the general structure of CBT will be the same for you as it will be for anyone else, the way it will feel might vary from person to person. As well, you might find yourself needing to slightly adapt the process and move at your own pace so that you can begin making a real impact on healing your depression.

The key to navigating depression with CBT is to recognize that while CBT provides you with a clear framework, the goal is always toward healing and helping yourself naturally and effectively overcome depression by building effective self-management and mindset skills. As you continue to practice CBT, you need to keep this in mind and use it in the ways that work best for you so that you can start to feel better. As long as you are moving toward something that feels healthier and safer for you, you will find yourself experiencing great success with the power of CBT and the skills that it has to offer you.

How CBT Helps Depression

CBT helps depression the same way it helps with any thought-based or thought-involved ailment: it teaches you how to regain control over your mind and direct your thoughts purposefully, intentionally, and in a way that supports your wellbeing. CBT is going to support you in healing your depression by helping you identify false and negative thoughts and intentionally replace them with healthier and more realistic ones. By being able to regain control over your thoughts, you will find yourself experiencing less depression because you will be perceiving and experiencing the world in a way that is less likely to lead to depression.

Remember that in CBT, the basis for emotional creation is perceived as being a five-step process: experience, perceive, think, believe, and feel. For depression, it is believed that the experiences you are having are leading to you to perceive the world in a depressed manner, which leads to thoughts and beliefs that support the development of depression. From there, you begin to experience feelings and emotions relating to depression, which can lead to continuous depression if you are consistently experiencing these same habitual cycles of experiencing, perceiving, thinking, believing, and feeling about your world.

When it comes to life, you are unlikely to be able to change your experiences. While you can have some control over what you experience, in many cases, a large part of our external world is unchangeable, and we will continue to experience it over and over again regardless of what we attempt to create, experience, or achieve. If you want to experience a massive change in your life, you need to focus more on your perception, your thoughts, and your beliefs so that you can intentionally create a mindset that supports you in having feelings that are not depression.

The way CBT works specifically is by building skills such as redirecting your thoughts, distracting yourself, developing resiliency, and intentionally increasing your motivation so that you can begin to take back control over your thought processes. This way, you can rewire your automatic perceptions around your experiences and begin to experience something more intentional and supportive of healthier thoughts and beliefs. As you continue to increase and use these skills, you will find yourself experiencing a far greater capacity to enjoy healthier feelings, too.

Learning how to interrupt and change automatic perceptions, thoughts, and beliefs is not entirely easy, so it is important that you understand this and be gentle with yourself throughout the process. You need to understand that your brain works automatically in many ways and that attempting to change your automatic thoughts and behaviors can be challenging since you are trying to change your subconscious mind at that point. I explain more about why this is the case and how to change your subconscious mind in my book *Emotional Intelligence for Self-*

Discipline, so if you want to go even deeper on intentional subconscious work, that is a great read.

As you continue engaging in CBT, you will find yourself beginning to regain intentional and mindful control over your thoughts around certain things in your life, which means that you will have an easier time changing your thoughts. Before you know it, you will find yourself experiencing freedom from your painful perceptions, thoughts, and beliefs, and you will find yourself moving toward healthier emotions as a result. The important takeaway from this is that even if you feel like you are not experiencing any changes, or if you are struggling to implement these changes, you need to continue committing to this change in your thought experiences. The more that you can continue practicing this, the more your commitment is going to contribute to you experiencing overall changes in your thoughts and beliefs. As a result, you will find yourself experiencing changes in your feelings and behaviors, too.

The Cycle of CBT for Depression

To give you a clear understanding of how CBT is going to work for depression, I want to outline the exact cycle of CBT for depression so that you understand exactly what process you are going to be going through. Having a clear framework for your CBT will support you in remaining clear and understanding of what you need to do in order to change your thoughts and experiences.

What Depression Looks Like in CBT Framework

As you already know, the CBT framework for developing emotions is this: experience, perceive, think, believe, feel.

If you were to apply this to depression itself, here is what the cycle would look like:

1. You experience something that your brain wants to perceive
2. You perceive the experience in a way that is negative or false
3. You begin to develop thoughts that are negative or false
4. Your thoughts begin to develop negative or false beliefs
5. Your beliefs begin to develop negative or depressed emotions

The entire foundation of how you arrive at negative or depressed emotions starts with you having an experience that leads to a negative or false perception in your life. Naturally, the problem here is not the experience you are having but the actual way that you are perceiving that experience and what that is causing to take place in your thoughts, beliefs, feelings, and eventually, your behaviors, too.

What Healing Depression Looks Like in CBT Framework

When you begin healing depression using the same framework of CBT, it looks a lot different. In this scenario, rather than everything happening to you as you passively sit by and experience it, you begin to experience things on purpose and allow yourself to experience changes in the way that your natural emotion creation process works.

The process of intentionally creating new thoughts, beliefs, and feelings using CBT looks like this:

1. You experience something that your brain wants to perceive
2. You perceive the experience in a way that is negative or false
3. You challenge that perception and recognize that it is negative or false
4. You begin to identify a healthier, new perception
5. You begin to develop thoughts that are healthier and more positive
6. Your thoughts begin to develop healthier and more positive beliefs
7. Your beliefs begin to develop healthier and more positive emotions

In this practice, you intentionally and mindfully take back control over the automatic thought experience so that you can experience thoughts that are healthier and more supportive of a positive experience.

Chapter 7: Planning and Executing Cognitive Behavioral Therapy

Now that you are clearly aware of what CBT looks like when it comes to healing depression, it is time for you to start planning and executing CBT in your own life. This is where you are going to begin developing healthy skills that will support you in increasing your mindfulness while also increasing your ability to mindfully take back control over your thought processes so that you can heal your life from depression.

As you begin to develop these healthier skills, you are going to follow the clearly structured framework of CBT so that you have a clear path to follow when it comes to healing these things. This way, you can begin to create a healthier life for yourself with intention, and in a way that is clear, easy to follow, and makes sense. It is important to understand the importance of following this framework clearly so that you are not confusing yourself or leading yourself astray with your practices. The goal here is to make everything clear cut and as simple as possible so that you can have effective and productive methods for facing and navigating your depression. This way, you are less likely to experience yourself getting confused or overwhelmed or feeling far too much pressure on yourself to follow through with your steps for healing.

You might find that as you go through planning and executing CBT for your depression that sometimes you make great progress, and other times, it is more challenging for you to follow the CBT practices. No matter what, you need to commit to meeting yourself where you are at and applying your new CBT skills to getting yourself through your depression so that you can continually practice altering your thoughts for a healthier emotional experience. The more you can commit to and understand this practice, the more success you are likely going to experience through it.

Step One: Identifying Your Unhelpful Thoughts

The first thing you need to do to begin engaging in CBT is identifying your unhelpful thoughts. Your unhelpful thoughts are responsible for creating your unhelpful beliefs which are leading to the development of emotions like depression. If you can begin to identify your unhelpful thoughts, then you can follow them back to the automatic perception that you have and the way that it is impacting your feelings overall. This way, you can start reverse-engineering the process in a way that will allow you to begin experiencing a healthier emotional experience overall.

To begin identifying your unhelpful thoughts, you should begin tracking your thoughts in a journal. Pay particular attention to thoughts that lead to you immediately feeling negative or depressed, as these are the thoughts that are directly associated with perpetuating your depression. If you are experiencing a more advanced form of depression, you might find yourself experiencing a seemingly large amount of negative or unhelpful thoughts that are leading to these emotions. In this case, just start by tracking 2-3 of these thoughts and the patterns around these thoughts so that you can understand what is creating them and what beliefs and feelings are being created as a result of them.

As you begin to recognize your unhelpful thoughts, you will find yourself being able to identify the cycles that circulate around these thoughts and develop emotions. This entire awareness and understanding formulate the basis for how your unhelpful thoughts are being created, so it is crucial that you take the time to intimately understand this process. If you find that it is too overwhelming or that you are having far too many thoughts for you to navigate, take your time and begin with just 1-2 thoughts. You may find this to be more supportive as you learn how to build and implement the skills relating to CBT and how you can use CBT to overcome depression.

Step Two: Identifying The Behaviors That Follow Them

After you begin to track and become more aware of your thoughts, you also want to learn to track and become more aware of the cycles that immediately follow your thoughts. Pay close attention to the exact beliefs you develop, the feelings you have, and the behaviors that you engage in as a result of these beliefs and feelings. For example, if you experience a friend not calling you to hang out with you but calling the rest of your friends to hang out with them, you may perceive this as you being left out and not being wanted by your friends. To your friend, they may have not invited you because the last few times they did, you said no, and they were afraid of bothering you, and instead were waiting for you to ask them to hang out. Your false perception of what

49

happened could then lead to you thinking that your friends do not like you and the belief that you are an unlikeable person and that people who spend time with you or around you are just doing it to be polite. You may then begin to feel depressed and unwanted, which may lead to behaviors of you continuing to deny hanging out with your friends when they *do* ask you to come out. This may make them ask you to come out less and less because they recognize that you do not enjoy coming out with them or that you consistently decline their invitations.

When you can clearly understand what your cycles are around your perceptions, thoughts, and beliefs, then you can begin to understand everything you are doing that may be leading to you feeling depressed. The more you can recognize and understand how you yourself might be feeding into your own depression, the more you can take responsibility for these behaviors. As you take responsibility for your behaviors, it becomes easier for you to begin to develop a willingness to change your behaviors as you realize that it is possible, and it is within your realm of control.

You can easily begin to track and understand your cycles alongside tracking and understanding your thoughts. Doing this all at the same time can help you clearly see how your own experience, perception, thought, belief, and feelings patterns are working so that you can understand how you can begin to intercept and heal them.

Before you move into the process of doing anything with your thoughts and cycles, make sure that you can clearly understand them and how they are affecting you. The easiest way to do this is to write down the stages of the cycle and what is happening for you during each stage. This way, you can clearly identify how these stages are impacting you and how you can begin to intercept the cycle and heal your depression intentionally when the time comes.

Step Three: Develop Skills for Changing Your Mind

After you have begun to create more awareness around what your natural cycles are and how you are cultivating and nurturing depression in your life through these cycles, you need to start developing skills for changing your mind. The skills you want to develop with CBT include learning how to identify the part of the pattern that is leading to problematic thinking, learning how to redirect your thoughts, learning how to adapt to new beliefs, and learning how to develop stronger exposure resistance.

For identifying the pattern with problematic thinking, all you need to do is look back on your journaled cycles and identify where in the practice you were experiencing the development of depression. Ideally, you want to identify the exact moment that depressive thoughts began to enter your mind so that you know exactly what you are dealing with in your mind. Typically, that exact moment is the second that you perceive something in your environment that makes you feel depressed, or that reinforces your depression. The process of experiencing your environment to having a feeling can be incredibly fast, happening in just a few seconds or less, so do not be distraught if it takes you a few tries to identify exactly where the problematic thought or perception is happening.

Learning to redirect your thoughts can be easy in concept, but challenging in action. Many people find that when they experience difficulty with their thoughts they struggle to completely commit to redirecting them. It can be challenging for you to redirect your thoughts when you feel as though you are constantly at the mercy of them, or when your underlying beliefs are serving the old thoughts and not the new thoughts. Taking the time to effectively sort through your thoughts and create new thoughts can be challenging, but it is highly necessary if you want to change your experience. As you learn to redirect your thoughts, focus on creating new thoughts that are completely unrelated to the original thoughts and learn to stay committed to these new thoughts. You will discover that as you continually focus on these new thoughts, you find yourself naturally forgetting about the old ones. So long as these new thoughts are healthier and more empowering, they can also lead to better feelings than depression, which means that you have successfully instilled one of the main teachings of CBT.

Adapting to new beliefs is imperative as this helps you restructure your cognitive framework so that you are less likely to believe the negative or false thoughts that you have been believing so far. When you take the time to adapt to new beliefs, you need to take the time to understand that you are changing the deep inner workings of your brain so it can take time for you to completely make this change. The key to changing new beliefs is leaning into new feelings (or committing to a redirect like in the previous skill) as well as engaging in consistency. The more you can consistently engage in thoughts that support your new beliefs, the more you are going to be able to support yourself in having a healthier belief platform which means that it will be harder to believe depressing thoughts and easier to believe healthier ones.

Lastly, you need to practice exposing yourself to things at a rate that you can reasonably handle. Rather than trying to expose yourself to everything all at once, practice exposing yourself to your triggers or the events that usually cause a depressed perception a little bit at a time. This way, you can begin to develop a tolerance toward these triggers and you can practice using and reinforcing your skills around CBT. As you continue to expose yourself to more and more challenging situations, you will be encouraged to work harder and harder toward growing your strength in these particular areas of your life. As a result, your CBT practices will become more effective, and you will find yourself having an easier time overcoming these challenging experiences.

Step Four: Learning to Intercept Unhelpful Thoughts

Once you begin to identify what the skills relating to CBT are and what they look like, you can start putting them to the test by learning to intercept unhelpful thoughts. This means that anytime you find yourself experiencing negative or false thoughts about your life experiences, you can start practicing identifying the moment it changed, redirecting your thoughts, creating new beliefs, and becoming more aware of this situation. As you become more aware of the situation with the negative or false beliefs associated with it, you want to do so in a way that helps you realize that this particular situation may be somewhat triggering for you in the future, too. When you can identify your triggers or the things that cause you to start feeling depressed in the first place, you can begin to identify what can be done to help you feel better. You will also know that you need to brace yourself for these particular circumstances in the future and build your skill and resilience up toward them so that they are less likely to have such a strong negative impact on you going forward.

As you begin to practice implementing these new skills, you will likely find yourself feeling resistant to or overwhelmed by them at first. You may realize that you struggle to really implement any of them and that you find yourself feeling as if they are not working for you. Remember that hopelessness, helplessness, and worthlessness are all symptoms associated with depression and that any thoughts you have around these types of subject matter are not ultimately true. Continue practicing implementing your new skills over and over, and eventually, you will find yourself recognizing differences from them, even if those differences are small at first.

It is crucial that you remember that you are working on changing some aspects of your brain that are practically hardwired into you and that you are going to need to take your time and let these new skills begin to actually change your brain. As you continue practicing them, however, neuroscience has proven that you will actually be rewiring your brain, so that it has a stronger cognitive framework that supports you in seeing your life in an even more positive manner. As this change begins to shift, you will find yourself consistently experiencing more and more positive shifts in your life, which is a reflection of those new neural pathways taking deeper root and really instilling completely change in your life.

Step Five: Staying Committed to Change

Once you have begun implementing your new change practices into your life, it is crucial that you remain committed to implementing the change. Many people find themselves wanting to immediately stop using their new practices, or reverting to old practices after a certain amount of time or change results from their changed behaviors. Any of these regression patterns are indicative of a natural brain at work, as this is your brain attempting to revert back to old familiar ways which are easier for it to engage in and work with. However, you must recognize when your brain naturally tries to regress and be willing to remain committed to your change and new practices anyway as a way to help yourself keep changing and growing in life.

Remember, you are responsible for your healing and your treatment, so you need to consistently be willing to put forth the energy and effort to keep moving toward your changes. If you are going to be able to have the impact that you want to have on your own growth, you need to be willing to remain committed. Keep practicing your new CBT practices every single day so that you can continue to allow these practices to rewire your brain and change your experience entirely.

If you find that you have fallen off the wagon at any point, so to speak, or that you have gone a few days with regressed thoughts and behaviors, you need to take your time and allow yourself to begin moving back on track once again. It can be easy for you to allow yourself to simply shrug off CBT or claim that it didn't work or that you are incapable of making it work, especially if you are already feeling depressed and demotivated. With that being said, it is important that you do not do this and that you instead find a way to commit to creating new behaviors in your life so that you can begin to experience true change. Instead of allowing yourself to shrug off CBT and continue suffering, recognize a few missed days as just being a part of the process and immediately get back on track with your new skills as soon as you can. You will likely find that the sooner you can get back on track and the more frequently you can pick yourself up from these missed behaviors, the more likely it will be that you will be able to heal yourself from problematic depression.

Step Six: Tracking Your Changes

As you begin to implement your new thought processes and changes into your life, you need to make sure that you continue tracking your thoughts, beliefs, feelings, and overall cycles. The more you can track your CBT framework cycles, the more you are going to be able to recognize whether or not your CBT skills are actually helping you with changing your life. If they are, you should begin to notice at least subtle changes around your feelings of depression. You might not immediately switch into not feeling depressed at all, but you might find yourself feeling hopeful that one day, you will not be as depressed as you have been.

With that to be said, you need to track your CBT practices the same way you were tracking your unmanaged depression. Start by recognizing what your problematic thought was, then document what you did about that problematic thought and what skills you implemented to help you overcome that problematic thought. Next, keep track of how effectively you applied that skill and how strong you felt with implementing that new particular skill. Then, go on to document what you felt like after and how those changed feelings began to support you with changing your behaviors overall.

Be sure that you monitor and document even the slightest changes in your mood, as these can help indicate as to whether or not you are moving in the right direction. Even if you notice a subtle and inconsistent change at first, it is likely that you will begin to notice more dramatic and consistent changes over time.

If you have a hard time knowing how to track these subtle changes, consider using a scale from 1-10 in your tracking journal. 1 should represent you being incredibly depressed with absolutely no hope and intense symptoms of depression, whereas 10 should represent that you experienced zero depression at all and that you are feeling completely healed. Tracking your progress on a number chart can often help you track subtle changes and differences in your mood more effectively than trying to explain it in so many words.

Step Seven: Reviewing Your Experiences for Effectiveness

As you continue implementing your CBT practices and skills, you need to make sure that you take the time to stop and review your journal to make sure that your experiences are improving and that your CBT practices are proving to be effective. If they are, you should be able to find yourself feeling better from your feelings of depression over time, even if you are only experiencing subtle improvements at this point. If you are not experiencing a strong change in your depression at all, you may need to adjust your CBT approach or work together with a therapist and a medical team to help you manage your depression more effectively. In some cases, CBT might not be strong enough to support someone in overcoming depression but may instead serve better as a secondary form of treatment to help manage breakthrough or recurring symptoms while something like medicine helps manage overall symptoms.

It is crucial that you regularly monitor your CBT practice to make sure that it has been proving to be effective. If you are not paying close enough attention, you might find yourself struggling and experiencing incredible difficulties that would better be faced with trained professionals. While it is your responsibility to heal, healing from depression is not always something that can be done alone, and including the support of your friends, family, and sometimes, a medical team is important. Making sure that you have adequate access to the guidance and support that you need is crucial in helping you overcome your symptoms of depression so that you can go on to live a healthy and normal way of life.

Case Studies of CBT Effectiveness

There have been countless case studies done on CBT and the effectiveness of this particular treatment method over the years. If you are doubting CBT or if you need more evidence to help you fully believe in and have hope for the effectiveness of this treatment method, looking over some case studies of people who used the aforementioned practices to overcome depression might help. Below, we are going to review three different cases where patients experienced varying degrees of depression and how CBT helped them overcome their depression and manage future bouts with greater levels of strength and resiliency.

Case One: Puerto Rican Adolescent

Valentina was a 15-year-old Puerto Rican adolescent who struggled with feelings of depression. Her family faced several challenges from the time she was very young, ranging from poverty to being exposed to physical violence, and this manifested in Valentina as major depressive disorder (MDD.)

Upon entering therapy, Valentina began using CBT with her therapist. At first, she struggled to make it work because she had high suicidal ideation and was struggling with a low self-concept. She also had highly dysfunctional attitudes which reinforced her MDD and made treatment hard for her. After 16 sessions with a therapist involving CBT and one family intervention, Valentina showed massive improvement in managing her MDD. By the time her therapy was terminated and the case study ended, Valentina had decreased the consistency of her depressive symptoms, dysfunctional attitudes, and suicidal ideation. Her sense of self-concept and self-worth also improved drastically, which supported her in continuing to manage and care for her mental health.

Case Two: 22 Year Old College Student

Jolene was a 22-year-old college student who was referred to therapy by friends who had noticed that she was dealing with difficult symptoms of depression. These symptoms set in after a troubling breakup she faced during the school year which leads to her struggling in her academic and personal lives. She came from a background of being an only child in a middle-class family that was considered "typical" or "average."

After being referred by her friends, she signed an informed consent form and began receiving treatment in the form of CBT through the school psychologist. The symptoms she started in treatment included: feeling unattractive, poor eating habits, lack of physical exercise, and excessive sleeping and binge drinking. Following 8 sessions in treatment with her therapist where they focused on CBT practices, Jolene began to experience a complete shift in her depressive experiences. Rather than feeling inconsolable, unattractive, and taking poor care of herself, she began feeling positive, optimistic, and confident in her appearance. She also started eating healthier, getting more frequent exercise, and reducing the amount of binge drinking she was engaging in on weekends and after school. She reported feeling significantly healthier overall, and this was reflected in a 7-point drop on the BDI-II, a CBT test that measures the symptoms of depression, after her fourth session. By her eighth session, she was feeling back to her normal self and was seemingly past the painful overwhelm and depression that followed her breakup.

Case Three: 40-Year-Old Corporate Employee

David was a 40-year-old corporate employee who had been working at a mediocre job most of his life. He was responsible for earning the majority of the income in his household, which meant that his job was incredibly important to his family. This only increased David's stress around his work. Aside from the immense amount of pressure from his family, David felt a lot of pressure to perform at work and, to make matters worse, he wasn't being paid very well or treated very well for the job he was doing. David began to realize he was depressed when he was no longer interested in spending time with his family after work but instead wanted to lay in bed and watch TV or go straight to sleep. When he did spend time with his family, David struggled to feel connected to them and frequently felt like he was feeling out of place in his own family. This lead to feelings of overwhelm, worthlessness, and a sense of hopelessness because he could not see any possible way out of the troubles he was facing.

Every day he went to a job where he felt forced to accept being treated badly and paid poorly, and when he came home to his family only to feel overwhelmed and guilty when he retreated to the bedroom without so much as having a conversation with anyone.

David's wife referred him to a therapist she met through a friend as a way to help him learn how to cope with the stress and depression he was facing, and so he started in therapy where they decided to try out CBT to manage his symptoms. The therapist said CBT would support him in overcoming his current troubles while also having an increased resiliency toward future stress.

Within three sessions, David was already beginning to experience less stress in his life and was having an easier time connecting with his family and feeling better at work. While his circumstances never changed, he reported feeling a lot more relaxed at work and a lot less bothered by the treatment he received there. When he got home, he was able to enjoy conversations with his family, partake in family outings, and spend more time around his loved ones enjoying their presence and company. By the end of six sessions, David claimed he felt completely unphased by the stressors at work anymore and that he was confident in the quality of relationships he was sharing with his family. He also started to build healthier friendships with his friends once again and began spending time alone intentionally engaging in hobbies rather than hiding out in bed or going to sleep because he was too overwhelmed to engage in life anymore.

Chapter 8: Creating the Ability to Change Your Mood

CBT has the power to help you in many ways, including changing your mood. Moods are formed through emotions that are not allowed to be felt and then expired, so if you find yourself experiencing a mood, this is because you are consistently holding onto feelings that are causing you to cling to this mood. If you want to change those feelings, you are going to need to change the entire emotional creation or CBT framework behind those feelings so that you can begin to cultivate a healthier mood on a more consistent basis.

If you want to change your mood, you need to enlist the help of CBT in a way that is going to remain consistent and supportive over time, while also helping you snap out of the mood as quickly as possible. This means that you are going to enlist CBT in two different ways: one that is preventative, and one that is transformative.

For preventative CBT, you are going to focus on creating the CBT framework for healthier perceptions and outlooks on life, in general, so that you are less likely to cultivate depressed or negative moods. This consistent work toward managing your beliefs and CBT framework will support you in avoiding developing depressed or negative moods in the first place. As you work on healing your depression, this is an important and effective long-term method for being able to overcome depression and everything that tends to come with it.

For transformative CBT, you are going to focus on how you can get out of a mood quickly. This is important if you find that you have been clinging to a particular mood and that you are ready to change out of that mood, as it will help you find a new way to approach your thought processes and experiences at the moment. Transformative CBT is not effective as long-term treatment as it will not help change your ongoing CBT framework, but it will help you change your framework at the moment so that you are able to snap out of an unwanted mood.

If you combine preventative and transformative CBT, you will find yourself easily being able to snap out of unwanted moods when they arise and adjusting your underlying management systems so that they are less likely to come back. The more that you can consistently work on applying these two techniques to your CBT practices and depression healing efforts, the more likely they are going to work for you.

As with any form of CBT or similar practice, understand that it will take time for these changes to fully take place in your life, so you need to continually practice them in order for them to make a consistent and effective impact on your life. As you continue to implement these, you will find that your underlying energy and emotions improve *and* that your immediate energy and emotions improve, too.

Preventative CBT Practices to Improve Your Mood

When it comes to preventative CBT practices to improve your mood, you want to go a step further than wanting to end your depression and into actually deciding what mood you would rather experience on a consistent basis. In this case, rather than saying "I don't want to feel depressed" you could say something like "I do want to feel content" or "I do want to feel happy." This way, you are more likely to focus on what you do want and you can take an effort in creating that mood, rather than focusing on what you don't want and settling for any other mood that might come along.

Aside from setting an intention for what you want your general mood to be like, you also want to make sure that you are focusing on creating strong CBT practices that are going to help you actually create those new moods. Redirecting your thoughts and committing to change are two incredibly important practices that you can use to help you begin to permanently change your mood in a more preventative manner.

Another one you can use that will be incredibly helpful is recognizing *any* experience that is taking you into any form of negative or unwanted mood and begin to practice CBT immediately. This means if you are feeling depressed, anxious, aggressive, overwhelmed, or anything else that you do not want to feel, you immediately begin to practice witnessing it and redirecting your thoughts to improve your mood. That way, you are less likely to succumb to your unwanted mood.

You can also begin to focus on creating habits in your life that support you in naturally creating the mood you desire to have without ever having to experience a shift into an unwanted mood to trigger these new habits. Learning to have more enjoyable morning routines, evening routines, or other routines in your life can support you in having a more positive mood overall. This way, you are not consistently swinging back and forth between negative and positive moods but instead, you are more consistently maintaining a positive mood.

If you find yourself struggling to maintain these new routines, you need to make sure that you apply the effort of consistency and continually applying your new habit no matter what. This is a skill I talk about in my book *Emotional Intelligence for Self-Discipline,* and I cannot stress enough how important it is when it comes to managing your emotions and creating a healthier resiliency toward things like depression. The more that you can stay committed to your chosen routines and habits no matter what, the more consistently you will be able to engage in them and the more impact they will have on helping you move past unwanted experiences.

Transformative CBT Practices to Improve Your Mood

When you find yourself slipping into a mood, such as a depressed mood, you will want to use transformative CBT as a way to prevent that mood from going any further. Transformative CBT is best used after you have experienced an ongoing emotion that is beginning to feel unchangeable. If you use it early on, transformative CBT will support you in fixing that mood before it carries on too long and creates a stronger mood that is even more difficult to shake.

Transformative CBT relies heavily on quick, impactful changes that can help you begin to immediately start shaking off a mood and begin feeling the way you want to feel again. A great way to begin using transformative CBT is to master the art of quickly deciding and changing your focus immediately upon recognizing that your mood has shifted into something that you do not want to be experiencing.

With transformative CBT, your immediate focus is less on what your problematic thought is and more on what thought and following action are going to help you move beyond your negative experiences and into more positive ones. So, if you find yourself experiencing depression, for example, and you notice that as the day went on, you became increasingly more depressed, you could use transformative CBT to help you shake your mood from that day. You would want to start by immediately thinking about a thought that supports you with having the type of feeling that you want to have inside, and then committing to holding onto that thought and similar thoughts to help you begin to shift your internal world. Then, after you shift your thoughts, you would want to practice taking action that helps you shift into a new way of feeling, too.

You would be surprised at how big of an impact you can have on your mood even through small environmental shifts that help you begin to embrace a new way of feeling in your life. For example, if you find yourself having negative feelings, you could use something as simple as moving from inside to outside for a few minutes, standing up and stretching, or enjoying a favorite snack or meditation experience to shift your mood. These quick, 1-2 minute practices can help you drastically improve your mood quickly so that you are no longer stuck in the mood that you have found yourself being stuck inside.

Once you transform your mood, you want to move into committing to your transformed move. However, you should set aside some time later on to review your mood and reflect on why your mood shifted in the first place. The more you can understand why your mood changed and what caused your mood to change, the more you are going to be able to find yourself becoming more aware of what causes your bad moods in the future. This way, you can prepare yourself in similar circumstances and catch your bad mood even sooner, meaning that you will further improve your resiliency and ability to shift out of bad moods as they occur. With that being said, do not review the mood until some time has passed, and you are far enough away from it that you will not immediately invoke the bad mood all over again due to your thoughts or beliefs.

Committing to Your Changed Mood

After you have begun to enforce preventative or transformative CBT into your life to help you begin to change your mood, you need to commit to the changed mood that you have worked toward creating. One of the biggest mistakes that people make when it comes to CBT is recognizing the change, and then immediately doubting it or reverting back to the unwanted way of thinking the minute they start to feel better. This regression is often caused by habitual thought processes and patterns, which means that they are not necessarily done intentionally or on purpose. However, they can lead to you immediately jumping right back into feeling bad again which, if you are not prepared for it, may lead to you believing that the CBT did not work. In reality, what you are experiencing is more or less of a regression caused by habit and the strength of your outdated neural pathways more than anything else.

Once you have found yourself moving toward your chosen new mood, you need to continue to commit to that mood. This means that every time you experience a new thought or belief that begins to attempt to regress you back toward your old or unwanted thought or mood, you need to immediately stop and recommit to your new mood. This way, you do not undo the work you have done and found yourself immediately shifting back into the unwanted mood.

Again, at first, committing to your new mood is going to be challenging. You might be surprised to realize how many different thoughts and beliefs you have that can support an unwanted mood, especially if you are in that unwanted mood regularly or you were in it for a long time. The more you practice committing to your new mood, however, the more you will continually overcome these unwanted, negative, or false thoughts that keep leading you back to the old mood. Before you know it, it will become a habit for you to move into the new mood and maintain it immediately, rather than a habit for you to regress back into the old mood and stay there.

It can take quite some time, up to a month or even longer, begin noticing strong changes in the way your mind works, so do not be alarmed if the first few times you try transformative CBT or any other "quick fix" methods, they do not work for you. These types of practices need time for your brain to recognize them, understand them, and habitually and strongly reinforce them in your mind so that they actually have an impact. As you continue using these practices, however, you will find that you can change your mood in an instant with just a subtle shift in perspective and shake up your routine.

What to Do When It Doesn't Seem Like It's Working

If you engage in preventative or transformative CBT, and it seems like it is not working, chances are you are not practicing long enough for an actual change to be made. At first, it could take as long as several minutes or even an hour or two, or longer, of continued effort for you to begin noticing any differences in your mood. It is important that you commit to continually trying no matter how long it takes, however, so that you can see improvement and begin to experience the evidence that improvements are possible. The more you can work toward consistently making these changes, the more likely it will be that you can continually create a better impact on your ability to change your mood.

The more you practice changing your mood with either preventative or transformative CBT, you will realize that this time to completion gets shorter and shorter until you can do it in just a few minutes, or even just a few seconds. With that being said, you will not achieve this total improvement if you are not committed to consistently putting in the effort to change every single day. If you are not committed, you are going to find yourself struggling to see any changes because you regularly let your brain off the hook and give it the opportunity and space to regress back into old patterns.

Another possibility that may be leading to preventative or transformative CBT not working for you is that you are not allowing yourself to believe in the effectiveness of these methods. If you find yourself doubting them or experiencing disbelief around the functionality of these practices, you will likely hold yourself back by creating the illusion that they are ineffective. The less you believe in them, the less you are going to be able to actually create change in your life.

At first, it is going to be naturally difficult for you to 100% believe in the power of CBT and everything that it can do for you. As humans, we need to experience things and see evidence of effectiveness within ourselves before we can truly believe in anything we are being told or taught about. With that being said, you do need to do your best to have hope and belief that CBT at least *might* work for you so that you can keep an open mind toward the practice and continue practicing until you make it work for you. If you continue to attempt to engage in CBT without your own genuine belief in the possibility that it could work, you will find yourself attempting to grow with a closed mind which is virtually impossible. In the event of you trying to grow with a closed mind, you will be more likely to notice all of the flaws in yourself and in your CBT practice over anything else, which will ultimately lead you to talk yourself out of the practice before you even begin to experience any results from it.

Chapter 9: Increasing Your Sense of Safety

When people are depressed, it can be incredibly easy to slip into feeling unsafe within yourself and within your life experience. Depression leads to incredibly painful and real thoughts within our minds that can lead to things like self-harm idealization or suicidal idealization which both can feel extremely scary to face. In many people, they claim that depression makes them feel like self-harm or suicide is the only way out and that they *have* to engage in one of these practices if they want to feel any form of relief from their symptoms. In others, they might find themselves feeling afraid of their ability to take care of themselves and grow more and more afraid of their decreasing ability to do things like feeding themselves or practice basic hygiene.

Some people claim to feel scared of the feelings of depression, in general and worrying that they will never feel the same again, which leads to them feeling unsafe within themselves and within their lives. If you experience depression alongside anxiety, you might feel especially unsafe because the symptoms of depression may worsen and stimulate your symptoms of anxiety. If you do experience anxiety, you might want to read my book *Cognitive Behavioral Therapy for Anxiety* which is a great book to accompany this one and provides you with all of the details on how CBT can be applied to anxiety. In these cases, applying CBT to both depression and anxiety can be incredibly useful in helping you restore feelings of safeness in your own life.

No matter what you are facing, it is crucial that if you find yourself questioning your safety or not feeling safe in your life that you take the time to address this. Not feeling safe in your own life, especially if it is due to self-harm idealization or suicidal idealization is an incredibly dangerous space to be in. Often, this is what can lead to depression becoming fatal, so making your feelings of safety priority number one is critical in supporting your wellbeing. There are a few things that you can do to support and promote your feelings of safety, some of which lie within CBT practices and others that are more practical than anything else. You should apply any of these practices as you deem necessary to ensure that you begin feeling safe again as soon as you possibly can.

Recognizing Unsafe Thoughts and Feelings in Depression

If you find yourself feeling unsafe, you immediately need to begin using your CBT skills of recognizing negative or false thoughts to begin witnessing what is causing your feelings of being unsafe in your life. The sooner you can understand why you feel unsafe, the sooner you can begin to restore feelings of safety in your life. Take out your journal and begin writing down why you feel unsafe and what these thoughts of being unsafe are leading to within your feelings and within your behaviors. If you have any thoughts relating to self-harm idealization or suicidal idealization make sure that you write these down and that you immediately contact your therapist to let them know how you are feeling. If you do not yet have a therapist, you need to hire one if you are experiencing a form of depression that leads to thoughts of self-harm or suicide, because these things can be tricky and overwhelming to deal with on your own. It is safer to have a team of people supporting you than it is to attempt to navigate these things all by yourself.

After you have recognized your feelings of being unsafe, you need to start writing down the cycle that you have experienced that revolves around not feeling as though you are safe in your life. This means that you need to go through the cycle of experience, perceive, think, believe, feel, and recognize what is happening at every single stage that is leading to and reinforcing your feelings of not being safe. The more you can identify what these cycles are, the easier it will be for you to understand your triggers and support yourself in creating healthier feelings of safety within yourself and your life.

Using CBT to Intercept Unsafe Thoughts and Feelings

Once you have witnessed where exactly you are not feeling safe in your life, you need to start using your CBT practices to intercept these thoughts and feelings. If these thoughts and feelings are *not* leading to thoughts surrounding self-harm and suicidal idealization, you can likely rely on CBT exclusively to support you with healing your thoughts and creating a healthier space within yourself and your life. If these thoughts *are* leading to thoughts of self-harm or suicidal idealization, you can use CBT to hold you over until you are able to get into the immediate care of professional therapists who can help you navigate these unwanted thoughts and feelings.

The CBT skill you want to use when it comes to feeling unsafe is the skill of redirecting. Often, when we begin to feel unsafe in our lives, we can immediately switch into fight-or-flight mode which can lead to you feeling extremely scared. This can quickly activate your anxiety and make it even more challenging for you to come down from these feelings of being unsafe, which can trigger a major panic attack and/or a massive depressive episode. Knowing how to safely and comfortably redirect your thoughts will support you with overcoming these troubling experiences and finding your way to safety and comfort instead.

When you begin to use redirection, you want your focus to be entirely on how safe and grounded you feel. Focus on what is going on in your life that makes you feel safe, comforted, and supported, and pay close attention to all of the assistance that you have to help you get through any feelings of unsafety that you may have. If you need to, reach out to someone and talk to them honestly about what you are feeling and then allow yourself to completely receive their support so that you can witness how safe you truly are.

Some people will engage in certain coping practices that allow them to feel safer when they are struggling with CBT, which may be useful for you, too. If meditating for a moment, praying, or visualizing yourself being supported and protected, or any other practices similar to these support you in feeling safer, do not be afraid to engage in them during periods of feeling unsafe. The more that you can engage your mind and body into practices that help you feel safe and that disrupt feelings of being unsafe or feeling anxious, the better you are going to feel overall. This is the best way to allow yourself to completely overcome feelings of being unsafe so that you can start feeling better and more protected in your life.

Creating New Thoughts and Feelings Instead

After you begin to come down from your feelings of being unsafe, you need to move into experiencing new thoughts and feelings instead. This can be done by cultivating habits and rituals in your life that support you with feeling safer and more protected overall, which means that you will be less likely to be triggered into feeling unsafe again in the future.

At this point, preventative and transformative CBT are both great practices that you can use to remove the feelings of being unsafe from your life. However, there is further that you can go to really help you protect yourself if you find that you are struggling with feelings of being unsafe on a regular basis. For example, you can begin to build up a list of people that you can contact when you are feeling unsafe, you can hire a therapist, you can attend a meeting with other people who have depression, or you can join a support group. You can also begin to spend time in places that help you feel safe, acquire a small trinket or item that helps you feel more grounded such as a necklace or a pocket watch, or begin journaling. Often, any of these smaller practices can help people learn how to routinely feel safe so that they are less likely to be triggered into feeling unsafe or unprotected in their lives.

Once you find yourself outside of the feelings of being unsafe and back into feeling safe, you need to give yourself time to reflect on what caused your spiral, too. Make sure that you are far enough out of it that you are not susceptible to immediately feeling unsafe again if you begin to ponder these questions, and begin to really look at what makes you feel unsafe in your life. If you can, you need to start healing these things in your life or changing the way that you approach them. If you find that as you dig into these thoughts or feelings makes you feel anxious or unsafe all over again, this is an indication that you should not be doing this work by yourself and that you should hire a therapist or someone to help you through it so that you are no longer feeling so unsafe in your life.

What to Do If You Still Feel Unsafe

If you find that you are still feeling unsafe even after practicing all of these different CBT and redirection practices, it is important that you seek professional help immediately. Depression is serious, and sometimes, fatal illness that should never be overlooked or ignored, especially when you are having immense difficulties navigating it on your own. You might be afraid or unmotivated to seek help, but trust that help is a powerful opportunity for you to make the necessary changes in your life if you are really struggling on your own.

For many people, navigating and healing depression on their own simply isn't a possibility. Isolating yourself can actually be a symptom of depression and an activity that can reinforce and worsen depression, so if you are experiencing difficulty asking anyone for help this may be because of the depression itself. Do what you can to push past these feelings of discomfort so that you can hire someone to help you if you need someone. This way, you can seek the professional help that you need to support you with healing the troubles that you are facing.

Some types of professional support that you might seek out if you are struggling with depression include counselors, therapists, medical doctors, psychiatrists, psychologists, members of your church or clergy if you are a religious persons, friends or family, or even a crisis line or an emergency medical facility if you are feeling particularly bad. Do not be afraid to reach out if you do need help because there is never any shame in asking. It is better to ask for and receive help than it is to deny yourself the help you need and suffer in silence. Remember that no help can be offered to you if you do not ask, so it is up to you to take the initiative and truly ask for the assistance that you need.

If you are someone who is diagnosed with some form of depression that requires medical care, it is especially important that you pay close attention to your symptoms and keep your team involved in your symptom management process. Sometimes, your symptoms might be the result of your medication and asking for help can ensure that you get support with adjusting your medicines as needed. Never stop taking your medicine without the support of your doctor or medical team as doing so can lead to an unwanted and intense flare-up in your symptoms which might be too challenging for you to manage on your own.

Chapter 10: Additional Ways to Naturally Heal Depression

In addition to CBT, there are plenty of other natural ways that you can focus on healing your depression. Often, the most effective way to heal depression comes from a combination approach that includes lifestyle changes, psychotherapy, and occasionally, medicines for people who find that lifestyle changes and psychotherapy alone don't help. Incorporating these additional healing methods can help you naturally begin to heal your depression while also improving your chances of maintaining a depression-free lifestyle following your healing.

Note that it may take a while to find the right balance for you, so you may want to practice balancing these different natural healing methods out in your life, as you begin learning how to take better care of yourself and your depression. You may find that keeping a wellness journal, separate from your CBT journal, helps you keep track of all of the changes you are making so that you are more likely to recognize what is helping and what is not. When you do implement a lifestyle change, make sure that you record how you have been taking care of yourself in that particular area of life and how you have been feeling about it so far so that you have a clear understanding of where you are starting from. This way, as you continue to track your growth and changes, you will find where your improvements are helping and where you might be able to further improve to support yourself with experiencing even more healing from your depression.

As you begin working on taking care of these areas of your life more intentionally, you will likely find that you experience a general improvement in your health overall, too. For many people, especially those who have suffered from something like depression, taking basic care of yourself can be challenging and not taking basic care of yourself can lead to symptoms far beyond depression itself. You will likely find that your general mood improves, that you have more energy and stamina, that your immune system feels stronger, and that you have a greater sense of vitality, in general, when you follow these practices.

Getting A Healthy Amount of Sleep

One of the most important things that you need to do when you are learning how to heal from your depression is to focus on making sure that you are getting a healthy amount of sleep. Sleep can rapidly become disturbed by depression, and it can get worse over time if you are not careful and managing your depression intentionally and effectively. If you want to improve the quality of your life and start helping yourself naturally heal your depression, you need to make sure that you are sleeping enough but not too much.

Not sleeping enough can obviously lead to you experiencing low energy and struggling to engage in your day-to-day life. This chronic exhaustion can lead to an increase in depression as you have to fight extra hard to try to make it through the day and you struggle constantly with symptoms of exhaustion. Likewise, oversleeping can lead to problems as well which includes reduced energy and symptoms similar to exhaustion.

The average adult needs between 7-9 hours of sleep per day, at most. The older you get, the less sleep you need. Ideally, you should be sleeping within this timeframe to ensure that you are getting plenty of rest and that you are not oversleeping. As well, you should avoid routine naps when you are depressed as they can lower your energy throughout the day. Instead, focus on how you can naturally boost and maintain your energy throughout your day.

Engaging in Regular Physical Activity

The flip side of adequate rest is adequate activity on a day-to-day basis. Being depressed can lead to an increased feeling of being fatigued, even if you are struggling with sleeping on a regular basis. This mixed with a lack of motivation can lead to many people with depression dropping their regular physical activity and instead finding themselves feeling too exhausted to engage in regular activity on a day-to-day basis.

Engaging in physical activity is going to support you in naturally healing your depression while also helping boost your ability to engage in a healthy sleep cycle each night. Exercising at the right time throughout the day can boost your energy levels throughout the day while also helping you naturally feel more sleepy at night time, helping encourage a healthier circadian cycle.

If you find that you feel too tired or weak to exercise too much, try engaging in something simple like a brisk walk or some yoga at home. These types of regular activity will help promote more energy within you while also boosting natural endorphins and hormones that support you in feeling happier and healthier overall.

Eating A Healthy Diet

Did you know that serotonin is actually made in your gut? Your gut and digestive system are responsible for a large amount of the hormones and chemicals that are produced within your body. Eating a healthy diet on a consistent basis can help you manage your depression while also encouraging you to experience a boosted mood.

People who are depressed often fail to eat enough, or eat excessively, and generally find themselves indulging in things that are not particularly healthy for them. Learning how to commit to eating healthy and maintaining a healthy diet on an ongoing basis can help boost your mood while also improving your health overall. This improved health can also reduce the amount of stress your system is experiencing, which means you are less likely to experience hormones and chemicals like adrenaline and cortisol which can reduce the production of things like serotonin and dopamine.

If you have a particularly difficult time eating healthier and maintaining a healthy diet, focus on making eating as simple as possible. You can easily pre-cut and prepare healthier foods when you are feeling more energized so that you are more likely to eat them when you are feeling low energy. If a friend or family member asks how they can help you, you can also ask them to help you in this way so that you have healthier foods on hand to eat as you navigate your low energy and depression.

Herbs that Might Support Healing Depression

While there is no guarantee that herbs or supplements can support you with healing your depression, there are some herbs that have shown positive effects on people healing from depression in clinical studies. As long as these herbs do not contradict any medicines you may be on or illnesses you may have, incorporating these herbs into your diet or drinking tea with these herbs in them may support you in boosting your mood.

St. John's Wort is often known as being a mood enhancer as it is a plant that has been used to support mental health for hundreds of years. With that being said, you do need to be particularly cautious with it as it is not known as a long-term healing method, and it can affect the effectiveness of antidepressant medications if you are using any. As well, people who are pregnant or nursing should not use St. John's Wort.

Ginseng is another great mood enhancer that can also increase your ability to overcome depression. As well, chamomile and lavender have both shown promise in helping calm people's moods while simultaneously gently uplifting their moods which can lead to improvements in managing both depression and anxiety.

Supporting Healthy Brain Function

In addition to focusing on your mood and your ability to eat and live a lifestyle that supports a healthy body, you should also focus on living a lifestyle that supports a healthy brain. Your brain is often where depression is said to reside, so knowing how to support the healthy function of your brain will assist you in being able to create a healthy foundation for new neural pathways to be formed as you engage in healing therapies.

You can support the wellbeing of your brain, especially through omega fatty acids. Omega-3 specifically is said to support your brain while also helping boost your mood and reduce the instance of depression. While some studies show that it may not target depression specifically or serve in healing stronger levels of depression, it can help support healthy brain function which is incredibly important when healing depression.

Maintaining a Healthy Social Life

When people begin to suffer from depression, they can often be found isolating themselves from their friends and family and cutting themselves off from their social lives. Depression is often seen as synonymous with spending copious amounts of time lounging around in bed or on your couch blowing everyone off and doing nothing. Except, it feels less like lounging and more like laying on the couch or bed feeling completely drained and incapable of actually engaging in life itself.

Isolation is a huge symptom of depression, and one way to naturally combat depression is to gently overcome your isolation tendencies. Spend time engaging with your friends as much as you reasonably can when you are feeling depressed so that you are less likely to isolate yourself and make your symptoms worse. Text your friends, call them or even invite them to sit and have tea with you if you are feeling too depressed to actually go out with them. You may feel like you are being a burden because you are depressed and low on energy, but it is likely that your friends or family will not see it the same way. Make sure that you are transparent with them about how you are feeling and the support you need and let them come over and sit with you, even if you are not up for much talking. Often, just having loved ones around and spending time with you can help you feel supported and cared for, which can help massively when it comes to overcoming your depression.

Enjoy A Healthy and Fun Schedule

One way to heal from and prevent depression is to enjoy a healthy and fun schedule that you maintain with the intention of helping you fulfill your needs while also having fun in your life. If you find yourself typically having an unplanned schedule that is full of spontaneous activities, a packed schedule that isn't organized, or one that does not leave enough time for you to do the things that matter to you, you may be more vulnerable to depression. Learning how to manage your time effectively will help you make sure that you are feeling supported and cared for by the activities that you engage in so that you can find your way to feeling your absolute best.

If you are not particularly keen on scheduling, you might find that the practice of having one helps you have something to look forward to while also minimizing the overwhelm that can come with not knowing what happens next. Make sure that you schedule in everything that you need to do with adequate time to get it done, and that you leave plenty of time before and after for you to relax and enjoy your days. As well, make sure that you fill your calendar with activities that you find fun and enjoyable so that you look at your calendar and feel a sense of excitement, too. Only focusing on what has to be done can increase stress, as it can lead to you forgetting that you can have plenty of time to do the things that you *want* to do, too.

Avoid letting your life be about doing the bare minimum and then sitting around watching TV or playing on your phone in between everything else. Focus on doing things that really boost your energy like exercising, taking a class, going on a trip, or spending time with loved ones. The more you can make these things a priority for you, the more you are going to enjoy your schedule and everything that you need to accomplish on a regular basis.

Take Care of Your Emotional Needs

In our modern world, it is only now starting to be recognized that we need to take care of our emotional wellbeing on a regular basis if we are going to avoid developing a mental illness or emotional problems in our lives. Learning to fill up your emotional cup, so to speak, is a great opportunity for you to allow yourself the opportunity to feel emotionally nurtured, supported, and expressed so that you can stop holding onto emotions and building unhealthy resentments in your life.

There are many ways that you can begin taking care of your emotional needs. From learning to express your emotions in a healthy and productive manner by increasing your emotional intelligence, to spending time engaging in things that help you feel the way you want and need to feel, you can do plenty to support your wellbeing. For example, let's say you are feeling stressed, and you need to feel supported and to feel relieved from the burdens you have been carrying with you for some time. Taking some time out to take a bath, meditate, join a yoga class, hang out with a friend, or otherwise engage in something fun and non-stressful can help create that relief and promote emotional wellbeing. The more you can learn to understand your emotions, understand your emotional needs, fulfill them, and express yourself in healthier manners, the better you are going to feel. This is a great way to both overcome depression and prevent problematic depression from coming back in the future.

Boost Your Mood by Helping Others

There is a popular saying that goes "if you feel like you can't help yourself, help someone else." This saying is rooted in the idea that we can forget our importance and our ability to help ourselves and others when we are focused too deeply on ourselves and what we need. What can happen is we find that we begin isolating ourselves, and we find that we begin feeling helpless and hopeless. We also begin feeling like we are not worthy of receiving help because we are not helping others, which tends to be a common trend. As humans, we like things to be balanced and even, and we hate being indebted to other people, which is often how we begin to feel when we find ourselves receiving favors but never doing anything in return.

If you feel like there is nothing you can do for yourself, do something for someone else. Take some time out of your day to support someone else in feeling better, or to help them experience a higher quality of life. Hold doors open, volunteer at a shelter, support other people in feeling cared for and healthy, and otherwise help by offering your service and time to other people. If you can, join an ongoing volunteer program that supports something that you love and cherish in your life.

The more you can help other people, the more you are going to witness the development of gratitude in others. As you witness deep, pure gratitude in other people, you will also begin to experience deep gratitude in yourself for your ability to help these other people. You will also begin to realize that you have a lot of power within yourself to help others, which means that you also have the power within yourself to help yourself as you need it. This realization can massively boost your energy and support you in going to get the help you need or engage in the helpful practices that you need to overcome your depression.

Practicing Meditation and Mindfulness

Meditation and mindfulness are two incredibly powerful practices that can massively support your CBT practice while also helping you relieve yourself from depression. These two practices are frequently recommended and talked about in therapy, as they have the power to help people quiet their minds, experience relief from mental and emotional pain, and mindfully witness the difference between themselves and their depressive symptoms. In CBT, mindfulness especially is helpful in allowing you to witness the moment you begin to have problematic thoughts and what types of experiences, perceptions, thoughts, beliefs, feelings, and behaviors are surrounding those thoughts.

Meditation specifically is not only powerful at helping relax your mind but has also been said to actually help reduce depression in patients who are suffering. Meditating for as little as 10 minutes a day can help you improve your mental strength and experience great relief from your symptoms of depression. If you have a particularly hard time meditating on your own, you can always follow along with a guided meditation from a platform like YouTube. Many guided meditations will also focus on overcoming depression or developing uplifting feelings specifically, which can be a great way to improve your mood and naturally heal your depression.

Mindfulness is frequently taught alongside CBT, but it can also be taught all on its own or alongside almost any other psychotherapy practice that is used to treat depression, anxiety, or otherwise. Mindfulness is a great practice that can help you start to become more intentionally aware of the pleasant things in life so that you do not feel as though you are constantly being exposed to and overwhelmed by the unpleasant things in life. The more you engage in mindfulness, the more at peace you are going to feel in your life, and the more you are going to find yourself feeling capable of overcoming your depression and any other symptoms you might be facing. You can engage in mindfulness through meditation, or through intentionally connecting into the present moment and grounding yourself in present awareness.

The Power of Gratitude

Gratitude has an incredible ability to help uplift our moods while also helping reframe our awareness and train our brains to focus on more positive things in life, such as the things that make us happy and grateful. Researchers have learned that a daily gratitude practice being completed for as little as 30 days can drastically rewire your brain and support you in having a healthier cognitive framework that is wired for optimism instead of pessimism.

Expressing gratitude is something that can become particularly challenging when you are depressed and can become even more challenging the longer you experience depression for. If you find yourself feeling depressed, you might find that you struggle to experience gratitude and that you are constantly noticing the things you don't like in your life, but never noticing the things that you do like. If you take the time to recognize what you do like by recognizing the things you are grateful for, you can begin to change this habit and all of the mental processes that lie around this habit, including your feelings.

In order to pick up a healthy gratitude practice in your everyday life, all you need to do is sit with your journal every single day and journal about 5-10 things that you are grateful for. Even if you are struggling to think of anything, take some time to think about the small things and don't be afraid to write down things that seem incredibly basic. Do your best to make them different every day so that you are not habitually focusing on the exact same thing, but you are proving to yourself every day that you have plenty to be grateful for. Even after you begin feeling better, you should continue engaging in this gratitude practice so that you are consistently uplifting yourself and incorporating this into a part of your preventative healing routine.

How to Maintain a Positive Attitude

Maintaining a positive attitude is important when you are healing from depression, but the key is to learn how to do this in a way that does not result in you actually repressing or minimizing the intensity of your negative feelings. Many times, you will hear people say "just be positive", and this can be annoying and unhelpful, especially to someone who is truly suffering from depression and who has been placing a large effort into trying to feel better on a regular basis. With that being said, being positive is important, but not at the expense of expressing and honoring the emotions you are already feeling.

The best way to maintain a positive attitude is to cultivate a sense of optimism within your mind so that you can see the positive side of things, even when you are experiencing something negative. The goal here is not to minimize what you are feeling but instead to recognize that your negative or bad feelings are not permanent and that they are not the only thing going on in your world.

Learning how to experience negative feelings while recognizing that good things still exist helps put your mind in perspective so that you can foster a naturally positive attitude that does not discredit the pain or validity of your negative emotions. When you do experience negative emotions, rather than trying to minimize them, feel them and express them in a healthy manner while also recognizing that they are not permanent and that they can be healed.

Healing the Root Cause of Your Depression

Many people are unaware of the fact that depression does not just "happen." Depression has a root cause, and that root cause can often be identified and healed if you take the time to understand what is leading to those feelings of depression in your life. The root cause of depression will vary from person to person, so it may take some effort and detective skills on your behalf to get into the foundation of what is causing your depression so that you can understand why you feel this way.

Some of the common root causes of depression include a poor diet, a vulnerable lifestyle, exposure to trauma, high stress, being surrounded by other people with depression, or having a mindset that fosters the development of depression. Depression might also be caused by chemical or hormonal imbalances or genetic factors, so it is important to talk to your doctor to rule out these possibilities when you are getting to the root cause of your depression, too.

When you can identify and heal the root cause of your depression, your other management systems become a lot more effective because you are no longer just treating the symptoms but you are also treating the problem itself. This way, you will find that you are more likely to experience total relief from your depression and that you are able to actually avoid your depression coming back at any point in the future.

Conclusion

Depression is a challenging emotional experience that can lead to a great amount of emotional, mental, and even physical distress for the people who experience depression. Learning how to navigate depression in your own life can be challenging, and overwhelming. You might feel hopeless and helpless when you realize that there are so many variables when it comes to depression which can make it hard for you to understand why you have it and even harder to understand how to treat it. With that being said, treating depression is always possible as long as you are willing to continually look into how you can treat yourself.

One of the best things you can do to support yourself in treating and overcoming your depression is learning how to cultivate skills that are going to support you with your treatment. The more that you can cultivate skills that will naturally help heal your depression, the more you will find yourself overcoming the depression you are already experiencing while also avoiding the development of depression again in the future.

CBT is a powerful tool that you can use to help you navigate your depression while also overcoming the troubling thoughts and symptoms that depression can lead to. The more you engage in CBT, the more powerful your treatment will become and the more likely you will be to find yourself creating the capacity to heal from the depression that you are facing. For some people, CBT will be enough to completely heal their depression. For others, CBT combined with lifestyle changes and the support of a medical team will be necessary for ensuring that the individual experiences total relief.

When it comes to using CBT in your own life, it is crucial that you understand that CBT takes time to begin working. While it can often create quick immediate changes, the true lasting change comes from consistently committing to reinforcing and growing these skills over time. This way, you are able to effectively begin to actually rewire your brain in a way that supports you with having improved mental and emotional health overall.

As you begin using CBT in your own life, you will likely find that at first, you notice next to no improvements. It does take a few tries for you to begin to reach the level of improvement where you can begin to actually notice changes within yourself. Then, it takes even a bit longer for other people to notice changes within you. With that being said, if you can at least muster up a small amount of hope and faith that this can work for you, then you will be likely to be able to take advantage of CBT and actually make it work for you.

It is important that even after you find yourself feeling better from your depression that you continue to engage in CBT practices and that you continue to take care of yourself properly. People who have experienced depression tend to be susceptible to experiencing it again, so continually improving your skills and supporting your wellbeing is important. You should also continue to maintain a strong support team around you and be transparent and honest with that support team so that they can help you as much as possible, too. This way, you are most likely to heal and stay healed from your depression symptoms and any other symptoms that may be troubling you alongside your depression.

Lastly, if you enjoyed *Cognitive Behavioral Therapy for Depression: Retrain Your Brain From Wrong Behaviors, Irrational Beliefs and Negative Ways of Thinking, Open Yourself to Life, Happiness, and the Freedom of Change* and felt that it has supported you in learning to overcome and heal your own depression, I ask that you please take a moment to review it on Amazon Kindle. Your honest feedback would be greatly appreciated, as it will help me create more helpful books for you, while also helping others who live with depression learn important tools for managing their troubling symptoms.

Together, we can support a brighter future where depression is more widely recognized, cared for, and effectively treated using healing practices just like CBT.

Thank you, and best of luck in healing your depression. And again, please do not hesitate to contact a professional if you find yourself dealing with problematic thoughts surrounding self-harm and suicidal ideation. You do not have to go through this alone.